THIS JOURNAL BELONGS TO

A PRAYER JOURNAL

DON'T WORRY

ABOUT ANYTHING; INSTEAD,

PRAY

ABOUT EVERYTHING

MY PRAYER JOURNAL

DAILY PRAYER

LORD, HEIGHTEN MY SPIRITUAL SENSES

TO SEE THAT WHICH IS NOT VISIBLE,

HEAR THAT WHICH IS NOT AUDIBLE,

SENSE THAT WHICH IS NOT TANGIBLE,

BELIEVE THAT WHICH IS UNBELIEVABLE.

TEACH ME TO SORT THROUGH

THE NOISES OF THIS WORLD,

TO HEAR AND DISCERN YOUR POWERFUL,

WONDERFUL, PURE, PRECIOUS VOICE.

WRITE A LOVE LETTER TO GOD

SPIRITUAL NOTES TO MYSELF

PRAISE HIM FOR TRUTH

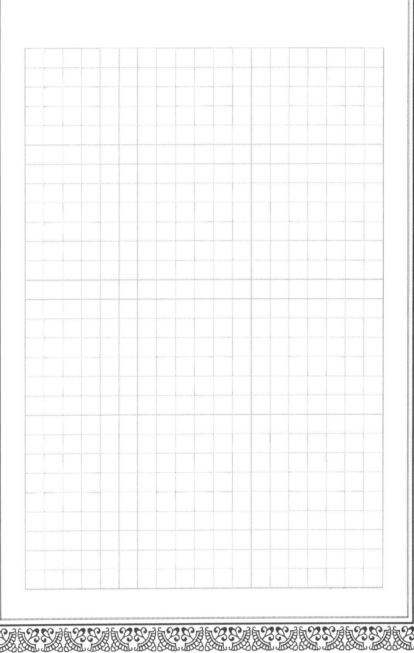

SPIRITUAL NOTES TO MYSELF

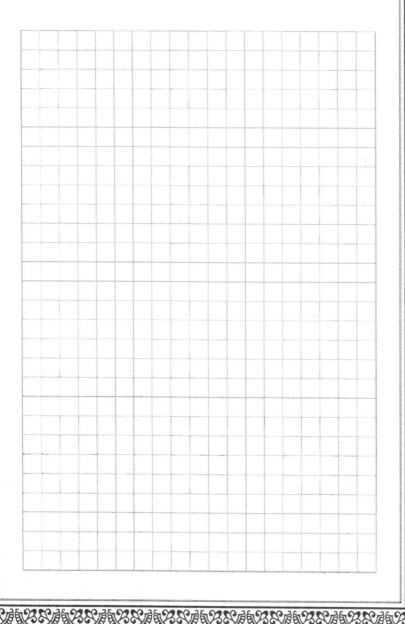

THANK HIM FOR A BLESSING

SPIRITUAL NOTES TO MYSELF

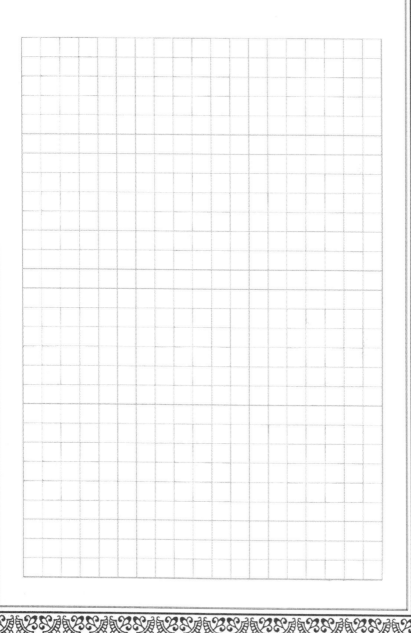

REWRITE YOUR FAVORITE SCRIPTURE IN A PRAYER

SPIRITUAL NOTES TO MYSELF

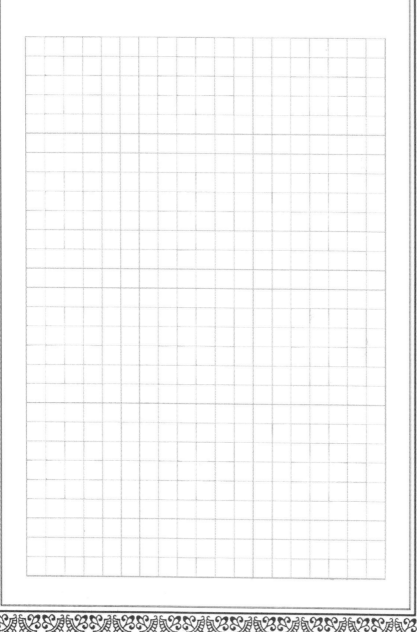

WRITE A LIST OF THINGS YOU ARE THANKFUL FOR AND PRAY THE LIST TO GOD

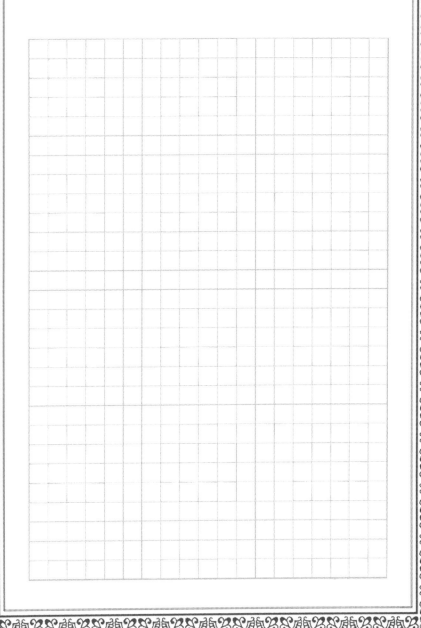

SPIRITUAL NOTES TO MYSELF

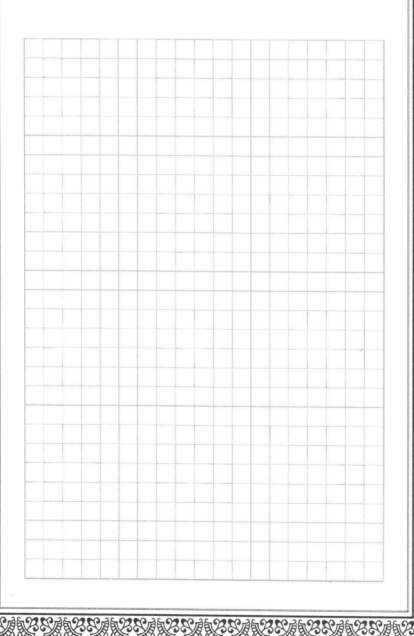

WRITE A PRAY ASKING FOR HELP TO FORGET THE FORMER THINGS AND STRENGTH TO MOVE PAST ANY AREAS OF STRUGGLE.

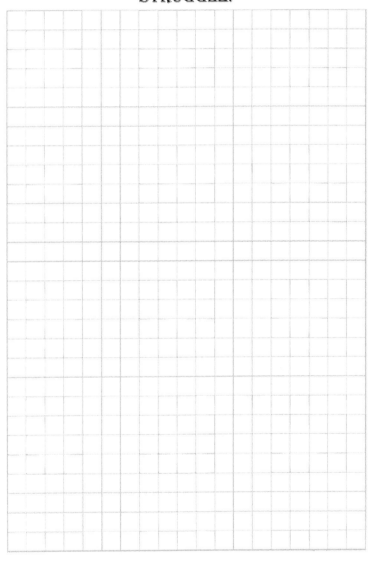

SPIRITUAL NOTES TO MYSELF

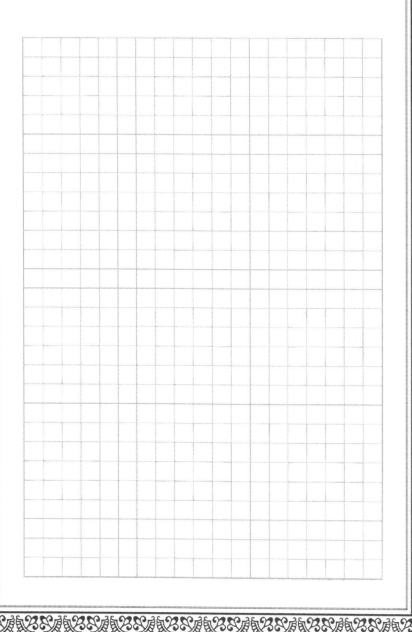

WRITE OUT A PRAYER IN AN AREA YOU ARE STRUGGLING IN ASK THE LORD TO HELP YOU OVERCOME IT.

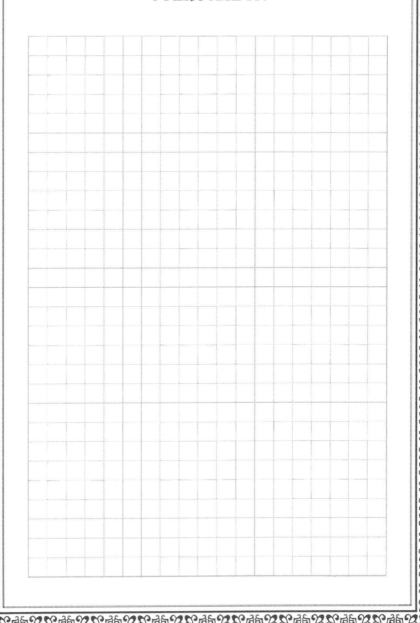

SPIRITUAL NOTES TO MYSELF

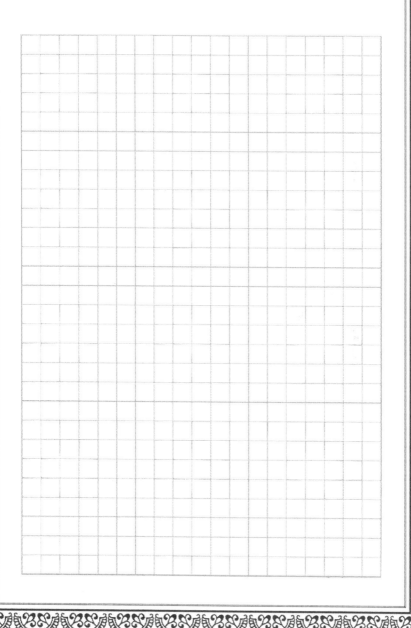

GIVE YOURSELVES COMPLETELY TO GOD

SPIRITUAL NOTES TO MYSELF

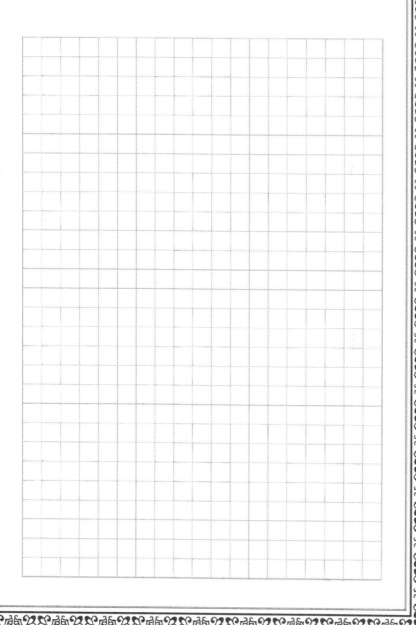

PRAY FOR YOUR LOVED ONES

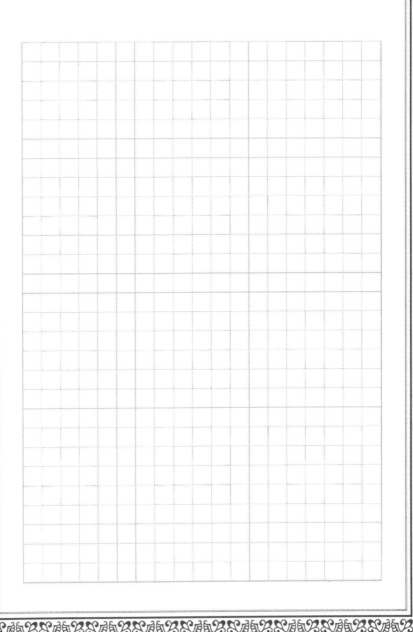

SPIRITUAL NOTES TO MYSELF

PRAY FOR YOUR ENEMIES TO FORGIVE

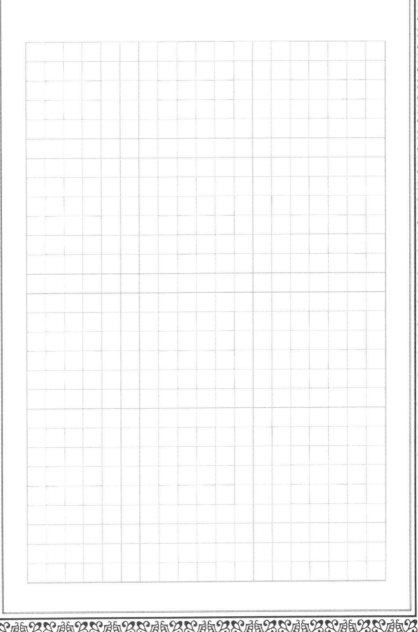

SPIRITUAL NOTES TO MYSELF

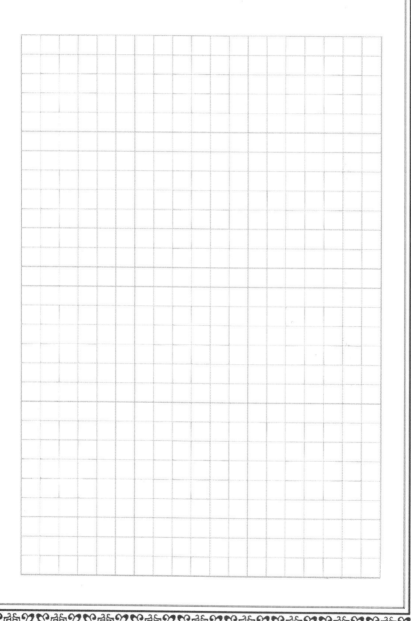

WRITE OUT A PRAYER FOR YOUR SOUL

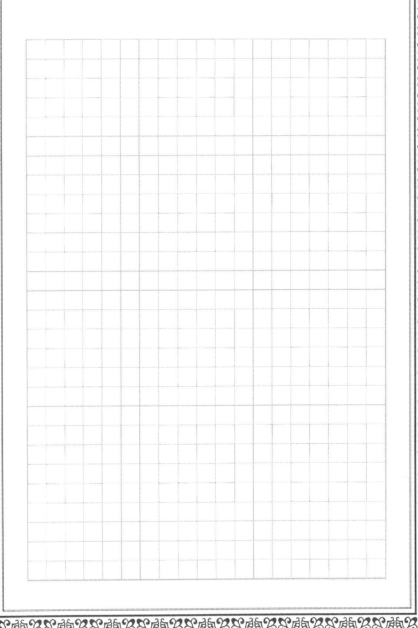

SPIRITUAL NOTES TO MYSELF

PRAY FOR THE WORLD (COMMUNITY & COUNTRY)

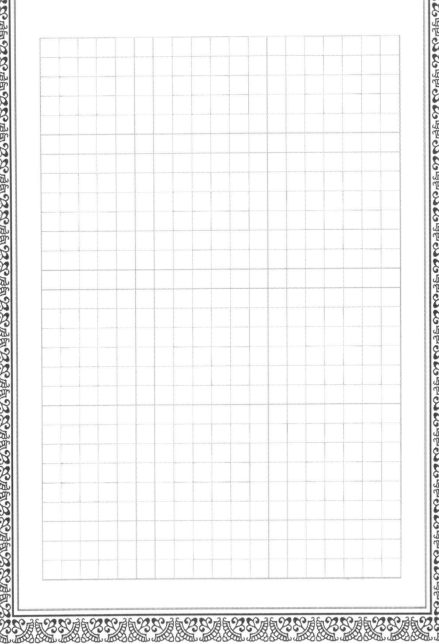

SPIRITUAL NOTES TO MYSELF

ASK GOD FOR WISDOM FOR WHAT YOU ARE FACING

SPIRITUAL NOTES TO MYSELF

WRITE A LETTER TO GOD SHARING WHAT IS ON YOUR HEART

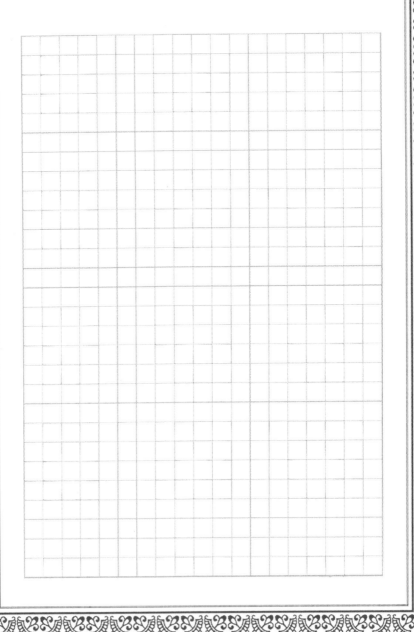

SPIRITUAL NOTES TO MYSELF

MAKE A LIST OF YOUR NEEDS AND PRAY OVER THE LIST

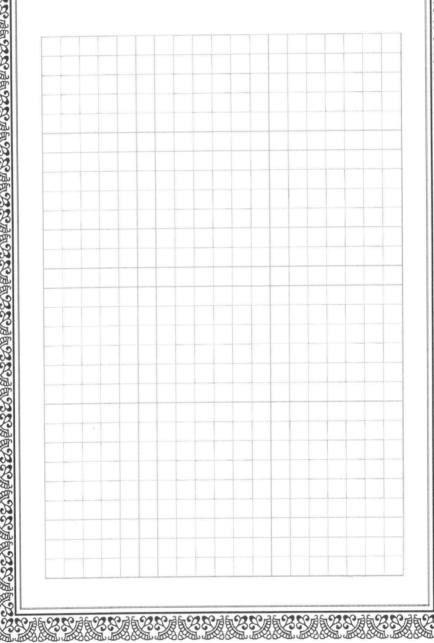

SPIRITUAL NOTES TO MYSELF

PRAY FOR THOSE YOU KNOW WHO ARE NOT SAVED

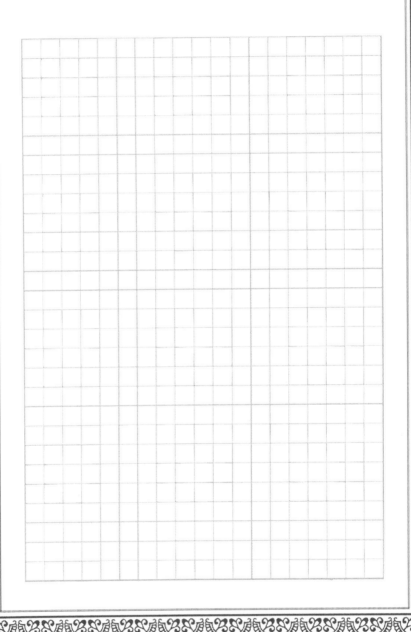

SPIRITUAL NOTES TO MYSELF

PRAY FOR YOUR PURPOSE, YOUR CALLING

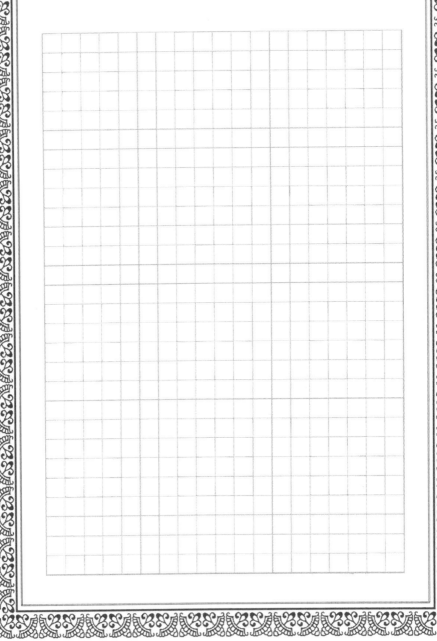

SPIRITUAL NOTES TO MYSELF

WRITE OUT THE LORD'S PRAYER

SPIRITUAL NOTES TO MYSELF

PRAY ABOUT HOW YOU CAN BE A TOOL IN

SPIRITUAL NOTES TO MYSELFGODS HAND

ANSWERED PRAYERS

SPIRITUAL NOTES TO MYSELF

ASK

AND IT WILL BE GIVEN TO YOU;

SEEK

AND YOU WILL FIND;

KNOCK

AND IT WILL BE OPENED TO YOU.

A PRAYER JOURNAL

Made in the USA
Monee, IL
06 March 2022

92347688R00026